# BOOK ONE

# A DOZEN A DAY SONGBOOK

## Easy Classical

Including music from Holst, Mozart, Offenbach,
Schubert, Tchaikovsky, Vivaldi plus many more...

Arrangements, engravings and audio supplied by Camden Music Services.
CD audio arranged, programmed and mixed by Jeremy Birchall and Christopher Hussey.
Edited by Sam Lung.
CD recorded, mixed and mastered by Jonas Persson.

Printed in the EU.

Order No. WMR101255
ISBN: 978-1-78038-911-0

WILLIS MUSIC

EXCLUSIVELY DISTRIBUTED BY
**HAL•LEONARD**®

Visit Hal Leonard Online at
**www.halleonard.com**

Contact us:
**Hal Leonard**
7777 West Bluemound Road
Milwaukee, WI 53213
Email: info@halleonard.com

In Europe, contact:
**Hal Leonard Europe Limited**
42 Wigmore Street
Marylebone, London, W1U 2RY
Email: info@halleonardeurope.com

In Australia, contact:
**Hal Leonard Australia Pty. Ltd.**
4 Lentara Court
Cheltenham, Victoria, 3192 Australia
Email: info@halleonard.com.au

This collection of well-known classical pieces can be used on its own or as supplementary material to the iconic *A Dozen A Day* techniques series by Edna Mae Burnam. The pieces have been arranged to progress gradually, applying concepts and patterns from Burnam's technical exercises whenever possible. Teacher accompaniments and suggested guidelines for use with the original series are also provided.

These arrangements are excellent supplements for any method and may also be used for sight-reading practice for more advanced students.

The difficulty titles of certain editions of the *A Dozen A Day* books may vary internationally. This repertoire book corresponds to the second difficulty level.

# Contents

Each track is split—hear both piano and accompaniment if the balance is centred, and the accompaniment only if the balance control is to the right!

# Jupiter

## from THE PLANETS, Op.32

*Use with A Dozen A Day Book One, after Group I (page 9)*

**TRACKS 1–2**

Composed by Gustav Holst
*Arranged by Christopher Hussey*

**Accompaniment** (student plays one octave higher than written)

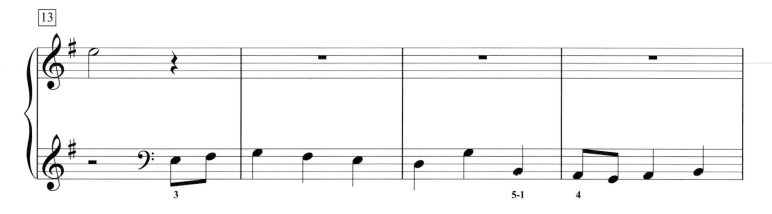

# Pavane Pour Une Infante Défunte

*Use after Group I (page 9)*

Composed by Maurice Ravel
*Arranged by Christopher Hussey*

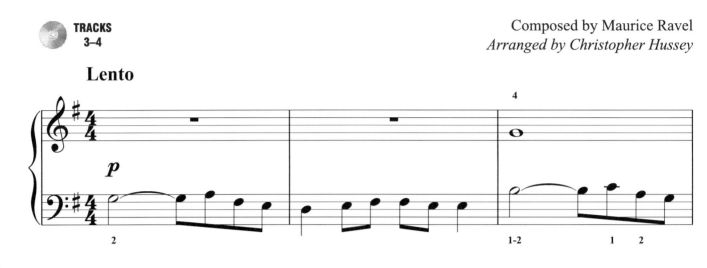

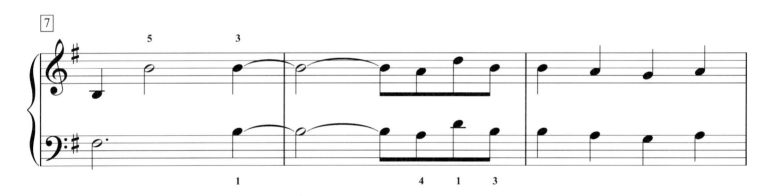

**Accompaniment** (student plays one octave higher than written)

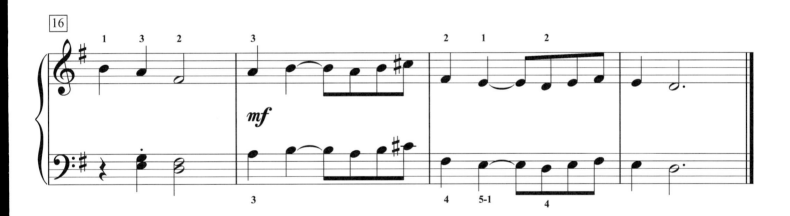

# Winter (2nd movement)
## from THE FOUR SEASONS

*Use after Group II (page 13)*

TRACKS
5–6

Composed by Antonio Vivaldi
*Arranged by Christopher Hussey*

**Adagio**

**Accompaniment** (student plays one octave higher than written)

**Adagio**

10

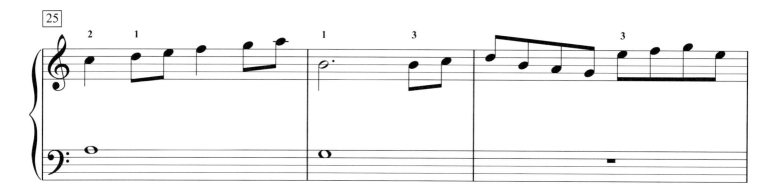

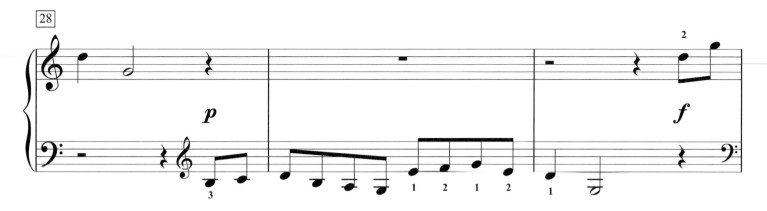

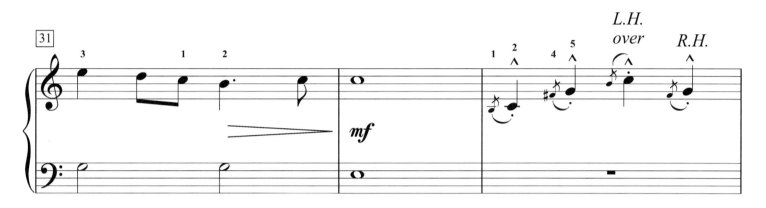

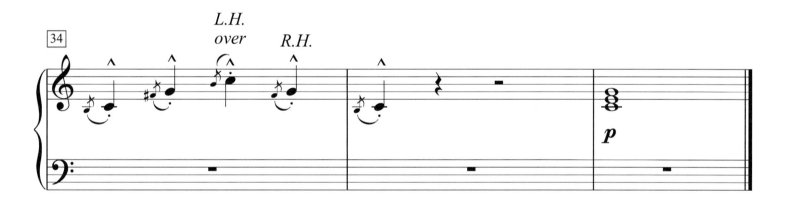

# Adagio
## from CLARINET CONCERTO
*Use after Group II (page 13)*

**TRACKS 7–8**

Composed by Wolfgang Amadeus Mozart
*Arranged by Christopher Hussey*

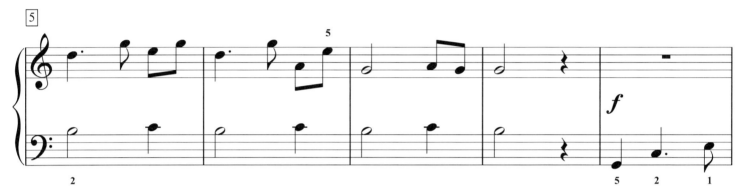

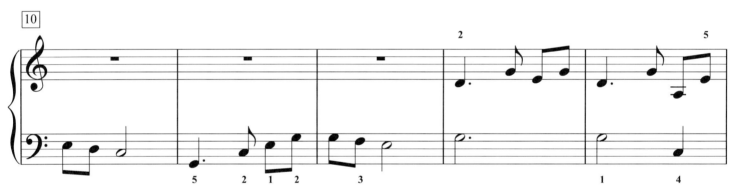

**Accompaniment** (student plays one octave higher than written)

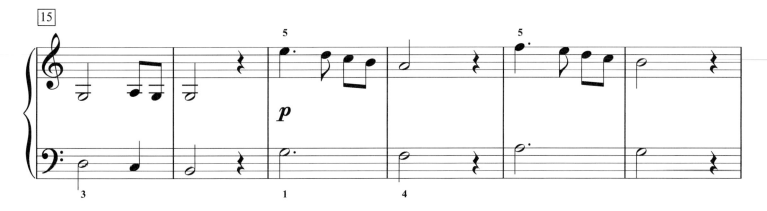

# Symphony No.5 (2nd movement)

*Use after Group III (page 18)*

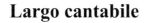

**TRACKS
9–10**

Composed by Pyotr Ilyich Tchaikovsky
*Arranged by Christopher Hussey*

**Largo cantabile**

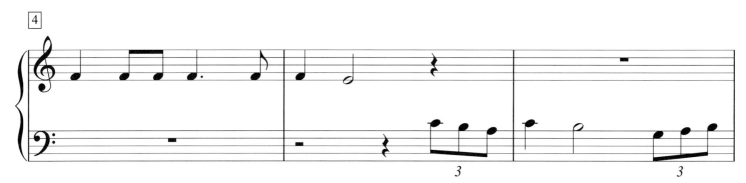

**Accompaniment** (student plays one octave higher than written)

**Largo cantabile**

# Jesu, Joy Of Man's Desiring

*Use after Group III (page 18)*

Composed by Johann Sebastian Bach
*Arranged by Christopher Hussey*

**TRACKS 11–12**

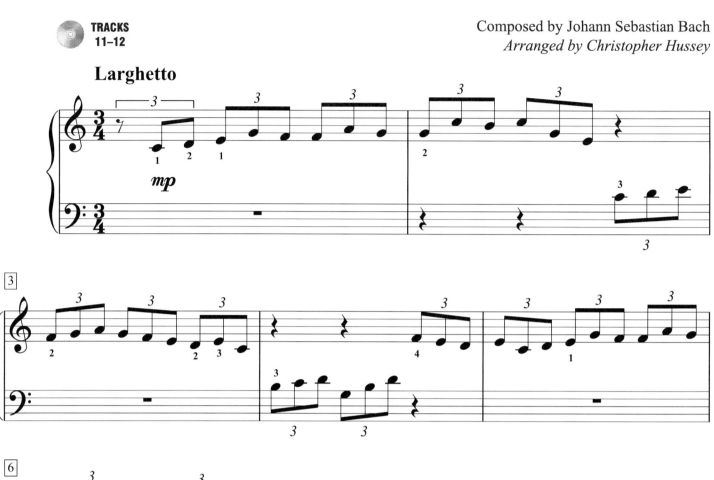

**Accompaniment** (student plays one octave higher than written)

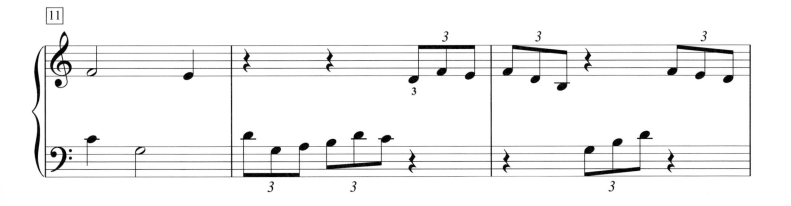

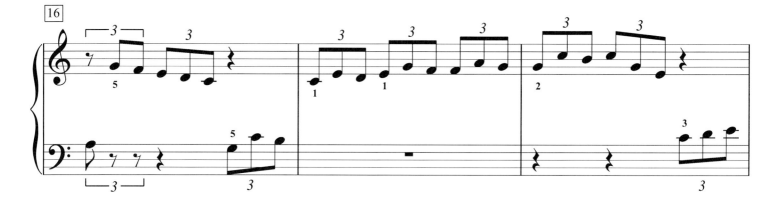

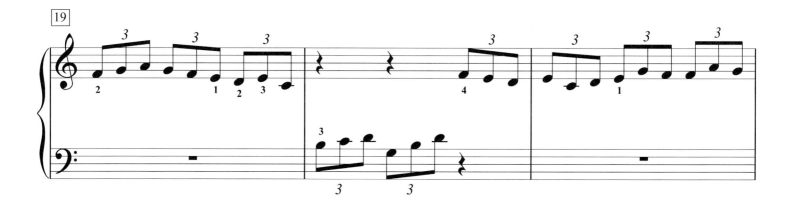

# Sarabande in D minor

*Use after Group IV (page 24)*

Composed by George Frideric Handel
*Arranged by Christopher Hussey*

**Accompaniment** (student plays one octave higher than written)

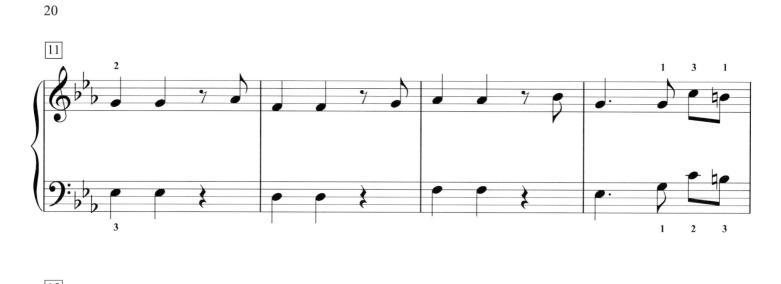

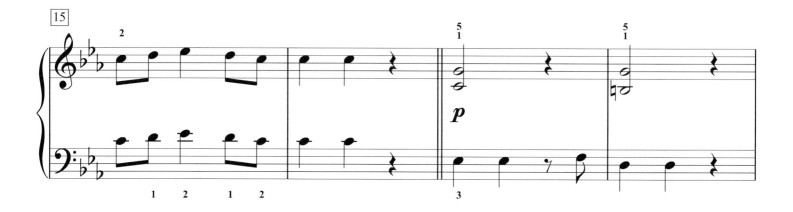

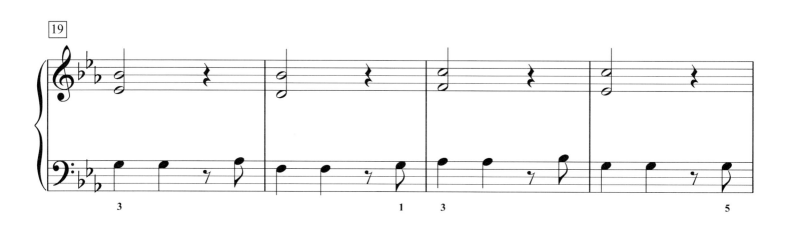

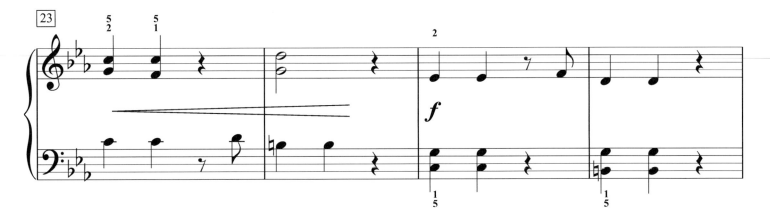

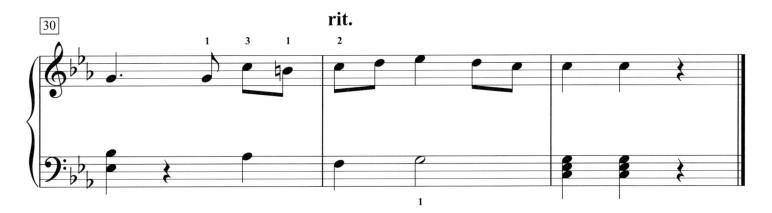

# Theme from The Unfinished Symphony

*Use after Group IV (page 24)*

**TRACKS 15–16**

Composed by Franz Schubert
*Arranged by Christopher Hussey*

**Accompaniment** (student plays one octave higher than written)

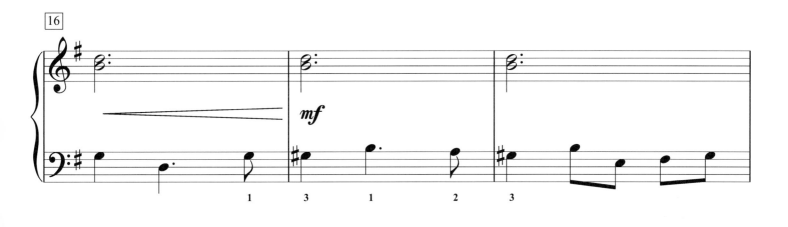

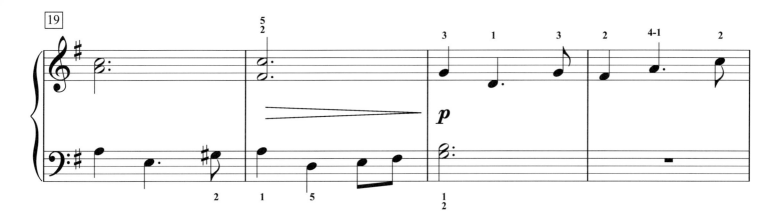

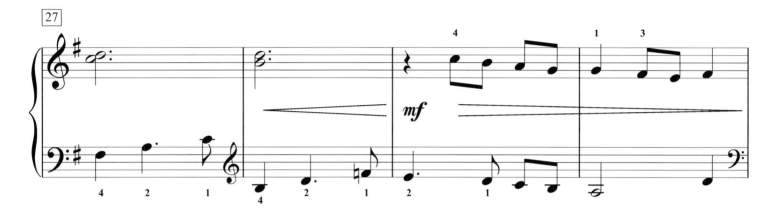

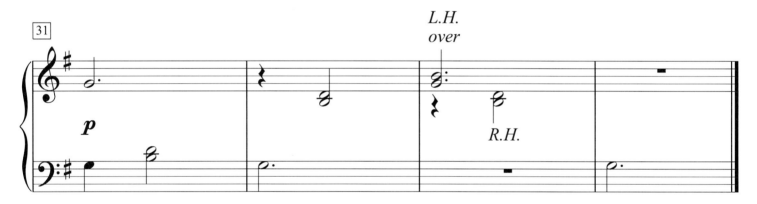

# Pie Jesu

## from REQUIEM, Op.48

*Use after Group V (page 31)*

TRACKS
17–18

Composed by Gabriel Fauré
*Arranged by Christopher Hussey*

**Dolce tranquille**

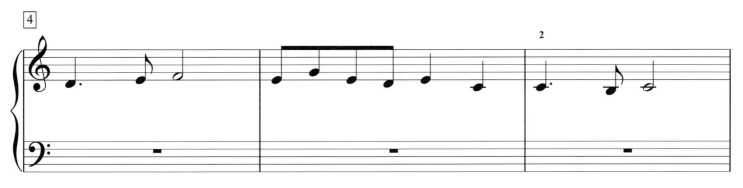

**Accompaniment** (student plays one octave higher than written)

**Dolce tranquille**

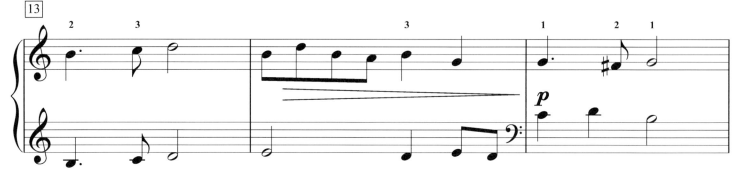

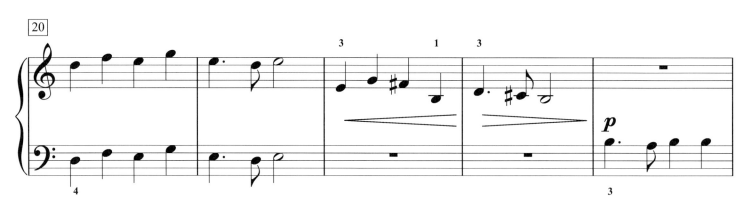

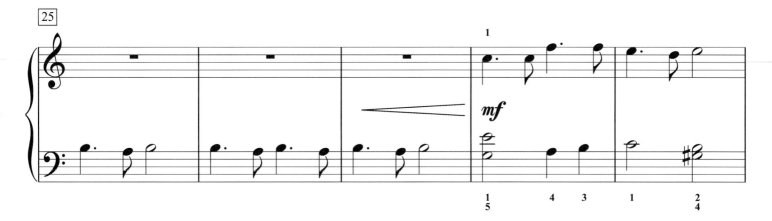

# Barcarolle
## from THE TALES OF HOFFMANN
*Use after Group V (page 31)*

TRACKS
19–20

Composed by Jacques Offenbach
*Arranged by Christopher Hussey*

**Moderato**

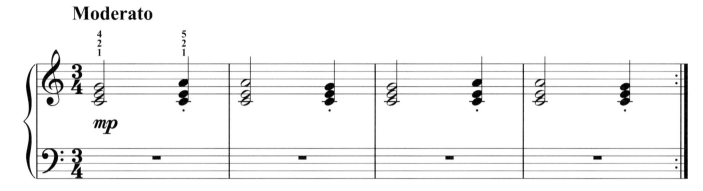

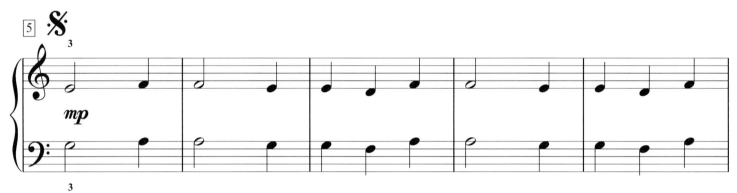

**Accompaniment** (student plays one octave higher than written)

**To Coda** ⊕

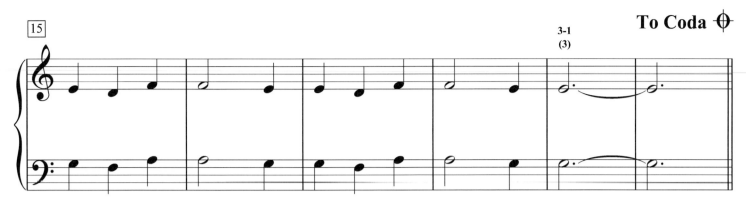

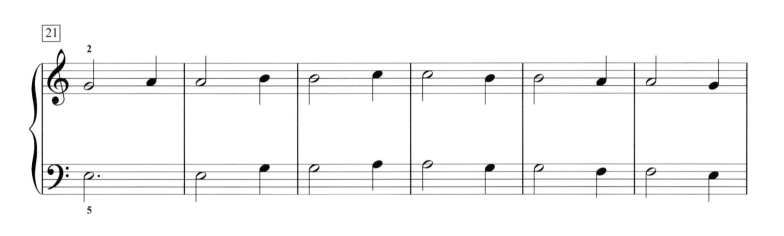

**To Coda** ⊕

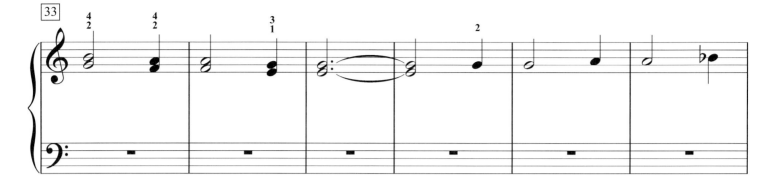

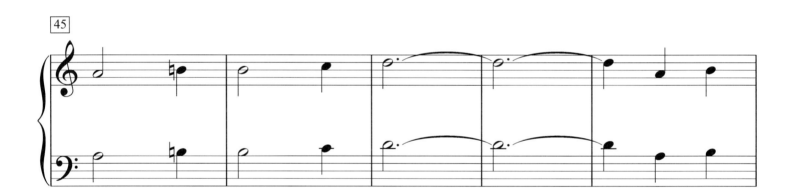

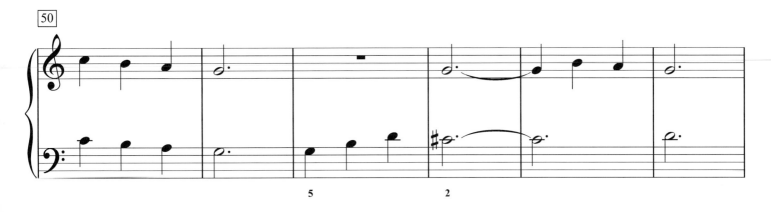

D.S. al Coda

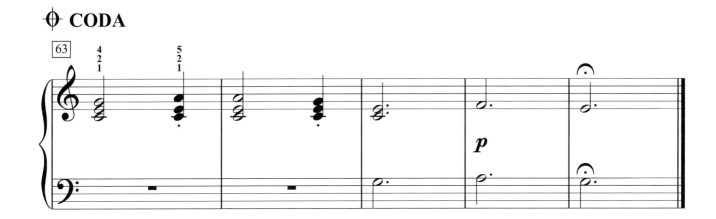

CODA

D.S. al Coda

CODA